X
612.8
ZIE
5/2014

D1243723

You Can't Tas

Pickle With Your Ear

AME

ST. MARY PARISH LIBRARY
FRANKLIN, LOUISIANA

A Book About Your 5 Senses

You Can't TASTE A PICKLE WITH YOUR EAR!

Harriet Ziefert

pictures by Amanda Haley

BLUE APPLE

A special thank you to Dolores Radtke,
science educator, for her
careful review of the text.
—H.Z.

To my faithful companions:
Brian, my husband, and Sally, my dog
—A.H.

Text copyright © 2002, 2014 by Harriet Ziefert
Illustrations copyright © 2002, 2014 by Amanda Haley
All rights reserved
CIP data is available

Published in the United States 2014 by
 Blue Apple Books
515 Valley Street, Maplewood, NJ 07040
www.blueapplebooks.com

Printed in China
ISBN: 978-1-60905-418-2

1 3 5 7 9 10 8 6 4 2

Contents

INTRODUCTION

What Are the Senses?

CHAPTER ONE

Hold Your Nose

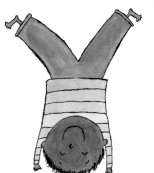

CHAPTER TWO

Please Don't Touch

CHAPTER THREE

Cover Your Ears

CHAPTER FOUR

Close Your Eyes

CHAPTER FIVE

Stick Out Your Tongue

CONCLUSION

All Your Senses

What Are the Senses?

Senses tell people and animals about the world around them. They warn them of danger. You use your senses to smell, touch, hear, see, and taste. Your nose, skin, ears, eyes, and tongue are working all the time, even when you are not paying attention to them.

When you go to bed:

- Do you see shadows on the floor?
- Do you hear your bed creak?
- Do you taste toothpaste in your mouth?
- Do you smell soap on your hands?
- Do you feel the covers over your toes?

When you do these things, you use your senses:

- You smell.
- You touch.
- You hear.
- You see.
- You taste.

Creak...

CHAPTER ONE

Hold Your Nose

If you hold your nose, you can't smell much. Try it.
When you let go of your nose, what do you smell?

If you smell food cooking, it might make you want to eat
something. If you smell something bad, you might lose
your appetite.

Some smells, such as smoke from a fire, warn you
of danger. Some are quite unpleasant, like the odor
a skunk makes when it is scared.

Deer have a very good sense of smell. They can sniff
the wind to smell if dangerous animals are near.

The next time you go out, use your sniffer.
What can you get a whiff of?

Dad drinks coffee.
Mom drinks tea.
Neither drink smells good to me.

My nose tells me
and it doesn't lie,
Grandma's baking
an apple pie.

When you're tired and think you're sweet,
Pull off your socks and smell your feet.

In her lunch box
Susie packs,
Salami, pickles,
and cheese snacks.

Wind and waves,
shells and sand,

The salt air smells
Oh, so grand.

Strawberry bubbles in my tub.
First I'll soak, then I'll scrub.

My nose knows
when Spot walks by,
If his fur is
wet or dry.

What Can You Smell?

- What can you guess from the smells in your house? If you follow your nose, can you tell what everyone is doing?

- What smells good to you? What smells icky?

- Does everything have a smell? Is there anything with no smell at all?

- Do you like the smell of flowers? Which ones?

- Have you ever smelled anything that warned you of danger? What was it?

- What's your favorite food smell?

- What do you smell right now?

CHAPTER TWO

Please Don't Touch

Hot, cold, wet, dry, soft or prickly. Nerve endings, or receptors, in your skin—especially in your fingers and toes—are always giving your brain information about the world.

Receptors tell you when someone presses hard, or gently, on your skin. They tell you when someone tickles the bottoms of your feet, or if an ant is crawling up your leg.

One of the first things you learned as a toddler was not to touch hot, and not to touch sharp.

By the time you were three or four, you knew pretty much what you could not touch, though even grown-ups make mistakes and touch things they wish they hadn't.

What can you safely touch?

Pat a kitty,
feel her fur,
If you're gentle,
she may purr.

Touch a toad, young or old.

Hoppity, hop, hard to hold!

Worms are soft, beetles hard.

Can you find some in your yard?

Baby likes banana
all mashed up,
Soft and mushy
in her cup.

What Can You Touch?

What's the softest thing you've ever touched?
The squishiest? The hardest?
The bumpiest? The coolest?

Have you ever touched anything that you
will never touch again?

Are you ticklish? Do you like being tickled?

Touch something with your fingers.
Then touch the same thing with your toes.
Does it feel the same or different?
What's the difference?

CHAPTER THREE

Cover Your Ears

Your ears pick up sounds from sound waves that travel through the air.

You need your ears and brain to hear.

You use your two ears to hear. Your ears hear sounds all the time, and you can usually tell where a sound is coming from.

Even if you cover your ears, some sound gets through. When you uncover them, you hear lots of different sounds.

Early in the morning—
an alarm clock rings!!!
A sleepyhead yawns.
A daddy sings.

What's that sound
behind the door?
I think it's Granny
starting to snore.

All day long on Maple Street,
Big dogs bark and small birds tweet.

Say "excuse me" when you burp.

When eating soup, please do not slurp!

Thump, thump, Mommy, come and see. A dinosaur is chasing me!

What Can You Hear?

- What sounds does your body make?

- What sounds can you make with your body?
  With your hands? With your feet?
  With your tongue? With your lips?
  With your whole body?

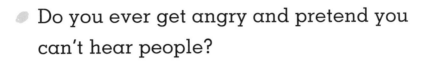

- Do you ever get angry and pretend you can't hear people?

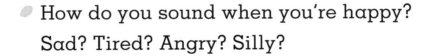

- How do you sound when you're happy?
  Sad? Tired? Angry? Silly?

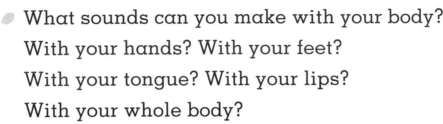

- What sounds from the outside world are coming through your window right now?

CHAPTER FOUR

Close Your Eyes

You have two eyes, which work together to help you see what is near you and what is far away. Your eyelashes and your eyelids protect your eyes from harm.

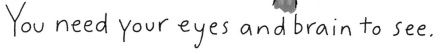

You need your eyes and brain to see.

An animal that hunts usually has two eyes at the front of its head. Animals that are eaten by other animals often have eyes at the sides of their heads. Chameleons can move each eye separately. This helps them watch for danger.

When you close your eyes, the world goes black.

And when you open them . . .

the `colors` come back.

Red and blue  make a **purple** cat.

Red and yellow  make an **orange** hat.

Stand on your head. Balance on your crown. Everything you see is UPSiDE down!

With an X-ray picture
All the bones

I can see,
inside of me.

Reading a book
about a pup?
Make sure to hold it
right side up!

A magnifying glass makes things **bigger**. Look what happens to a tiny chigger.

Magic mirror on the wall. Who's the fairest of them all?

What Can You See?

- What kinds of things can you see through?
  What can't you see through?

- Have you ever worn a blindfold?
  What does it feel like?

- When you shut your eyes, what happens
  to your eyeballs? Are they still?
  Do they move?

- Can you see in the dark? How well?

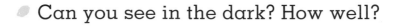

- If you put something in water and look at it
  from the top, does it look bigger or smaller?

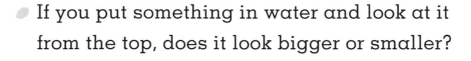

- If you put something behind a glass of water
  and you look through the glass, what happens?

CHAPTER FIVE

Stick Out Your Tongue

Your tongue has two important jobs. It helps you shape words so you can talk. It also allows you to taste, swallow, and eat.

There are groups of taste buds on different parts of the tongue.

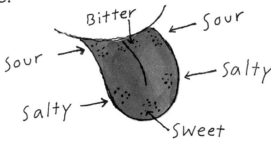

When you put something into your mouth, your tongue feels whether it is hard or soft, hot or cold. This means your tongue has both taste and touch receptors.

Just as the senses touch and taste are connected, so are taste and smell. If you stick out your tongue and hold your nose, it's hard to taste the difference between chocolate or vanilla ice cream.

But you if hold your nose and try to taste something sour, like a lemon, or salty, like pretzels, you may still be able to recognize them.

Lemons are sour; honey is sweet.

Which do you prefer to eat?

Oatmeal, custard...
thick, thick, thick!
Lollipops, ice cream...
lick, lick, lick!

This nasty medicine
makes me frown.
I'll hold my nose
and swallow it down.

Pigs are eating
all that slop.
If I tried it,
I'd throw-op!

How do you do it, Mr. Raccoon,
Eatin' garbage by the light of the moon?

What Can You Taste?

What's the saltiest thing you know?
The sourest? The sweetest? The most bitter?

Make a list of the spices in your kitchen.
Do you know how they all taste?

Taste: apple, onion, potato chip, banana, peanut butter.
Hold your nose and taste them again.
What's the difference?

What is your favorite food? What's your least favorite?
Is there anything you have refused to taste? Why?

Have you ever tasted anything you were sorry about?
What was it? And what happened?

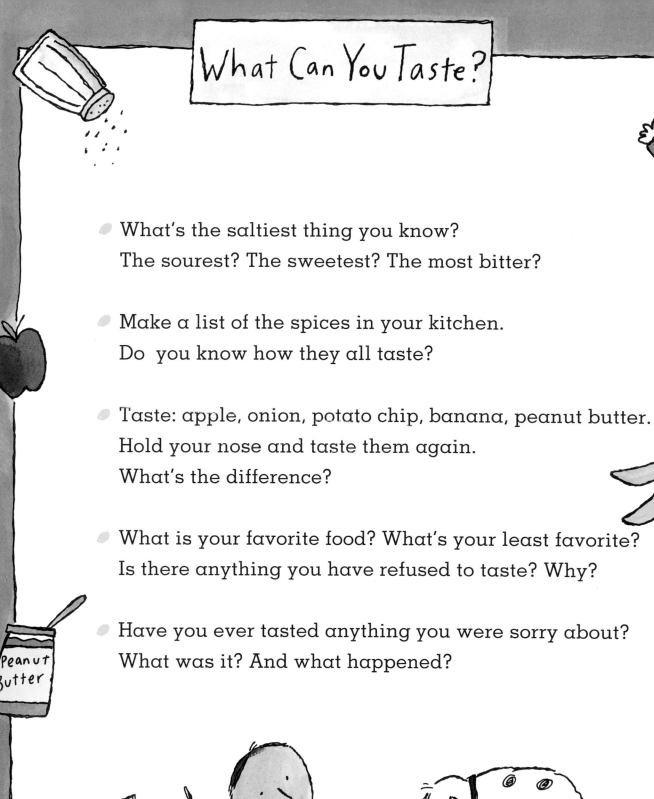

CONCLUSION

All Your Senses?

The senses of many animals
are better than your senses.
A dog can smell things
that you cannot smell.

A bat can hear things you cannot hear.

An owl can see better in the dark.

But our brains are able to use the information
from our senses differently from animals.

When you wake up in the morning and throw
off the covers, which senses are you using?

Our senses are important to us. We're lucky to be able to use all of them all the time.